WRITE ON:
THE 3'S OF PLOTTING

WRITE ON: THE 3'S OF PLOTTING

Published by Chapman Brown Books
Copyright © 2013 S.D. Brown
All rights reserved.

ISBN: 1494239949
ISBN-13: 978-1494239947

WRITE ON: The 3's of Plotting

S.D. BROWN

Chapman Brown Books

TABLE OF CONTENTS

INTRODUCTION

The purpose of this workbook is to give you a quick start on plotting your story. Before you throw up your hands and say, "I don't believe in anything that sounds like an outline," just give me a minute of your time.

Would you take a trip to visit an old friend in a strange town without consulting a map? You might, but you might not end up where you wanted to go. AND even if you did, you'd probably waste a lot of time taking wrong turns and end up backtracking. I'm the first one to admit, I love a spontaneous adventure, but when I'm writing, I can't afford it. Not if I want to finish the project in a reasonable amount of time. I speak from experience.

I used get a fantastic idea and just start writing. My story would go great for about a third of the way and then I'd get stuck, because I really didn't know where I was headed. After several "weak fixes" I'd struggle on and then come up with the perfect solution. The problem was that the "new fantastic idea" had a ripple effect like a tsunami in reverse. I'd have to go back to page one and rewrite. Losing characters. Adding new characters. Changing settings. Deleting scenes that didn't fit anymore. Writing new scenes that did. And. And. And. And it didn't just happen once, but three or four times. All on the same manuscript.

This guide is to help you avoid the waste-of-time-rewriting syndrome. That is, unless you just like to write to avoid doing the dishes or mowing the lawn and don't care if you finish a project or end up with a good story. With a little pre-planning you can "write easier" and "write smarter."

The plotting advice in this workbook is designed to help you streamline your writing. It's advice you can try, adapt or even ignore. It won't write your book. It won't control your voice. It won't spell out every detail. Like consulting that road map, it will help you to know where and when to turn, what roads to take and to know where you're headed. A plot plan, like a map, doesn't dictate where you stop to eat or who's tailgating you.

Good luck & happy plotting,

S.D. Brown

P.S. Feel free to write in this workbook or to photocopy the pages so you can use them again and again for your own personal use.

"The profession of book-writing makes horse racing seem like a solid, stable business."

John Steinbeck
1902 – 1968

THERE ARE NO RULES FOR WRITING, BUT THE ONES THAT WORK FOR YOU...

I've attended several workshops led by highly successful writers, agents and editors. All had different approaches to writing. What worked for one was totally opposite of what worked for another. Being a willing guinea pig, I tried several things that did not work for me. Like the time I wrote a "book of notes" about my main character before I started on the manuscript. I knew everything about her, from her favorite food to what she had hidden in the back of her closet. Unfortunately when I actually started to write, the shy quiet girlie-girl I'd planned was a snarky, spunky tomboy. All my pre-character planning ended in the trash.

Does this mean I never write up notes about my character? No it does not, but I don't write character notes until I've met him or her on the page. I write the first few pages of my manuscript first before I write my character notes.

The moral of the story is, you have to figure out what works best for you.

The exercises included in this workbook are the things that work for me. Hopefully they'll work for you, too.

NOTHING IS SET IN STONE. FIGURE OUT WHAT WORKS FOR YOU.

And as you work through the exercises, remember that they are meant as guides. Some of the exercises should prove invaluable. Some may seem to be pointless and a waste of time. The important thing is that you won't know which will prove useful unless

you give it a try. You might even want to adapt them
once you've tried them.

**BUT REMEMBER,
IF YOU WANT TO WRITE A BOOK,
YOU HAVE TO WRITE!**

1 PAGE A DAY = 365 PAGES A YEAR

**"UNLESS YOU WRITE THE SAME PAGE
OVER AND OVER."**

**ELIZABETH GEORGE
MAUI WRITERS CONFERENCE**

THREE IMPORTANT QUESTIONS

Before you start writing any story, there are three important questions you have to ask and answer before you start writing.

ONE, why are you writing this story?
TWO, who are you writing this story for?
THREE, what kind of a story is it?

ONE: Why are you writing this story?

The answer I'm not looking for is "rich and famous." What you need to know before you start writing any story is the reason you want to write it. Do you want to right a wrong? Expose political corruption? Do you want to change the world? Save the planet? Make people want to live moral lives? Or are you simply trying to write a great story that will expose them to new ideas and entertain your readers? If your answer is "yes" to any of these questions, except for the last one, you have made your job more difficult. Most readers like learning and/or being exposed to new ideas, but they don't like being lectured. And they don't like being manipulated to change their viewpoints. Most fiction readers read to be entertained.

TWO: Who are you writing this story for?

You wouldn't write a story about an accountant on Wall Street if you were writing a story for a kindergartner. Why not? The answer should be obvious. Most five year-olds couldn't care less about Wall Street or business accountants UNLESS it was a funny book about numbers where your kid character's father is an accountant working on Wall Street and only can talk in numbers. With some clever writing, it could be fun. Still, it should be the kid's story-view not the accountant's.

THREE: What kind of story is this?

Are you writing a mystery? Or maybe a romance? Science fiction? Political thriller? Fantasy? Historical? Or? Or? Or? It's easiest to write in the genre you enjoy reading.

Think about the story you want to write (and maybe have already started). Use the space beneath each question to write a short and concise answer. Keep in mind that all three answers should work together and not be at odds.

✎ YOUR TURN

WHY ARE YOU WRITING THIS STORY?

WHO DO YOU WANT TO READ IT?

WHAT KIND OF STORY IS IT?

"If writers were good businessmen,
they'd have too much sense
to be writers."

Irvin S. Cobb
1876 – 1944

THE BEGINNING Part One
SET UP THE STORY

The story should start with an incident that will change the protagonist's life forever and nothing will ever be the same.

The beginning takes up about the first quarter of your story. You introduce the reader to the "who, where and when" of your tale. Plus you present the characters, the protagonist's personal problems and the major conflicts that drive the story.

1.1 Characters - the "who"
Protagonist (main character)

This is the main character, the hero of the story. If you're writing for children, kids like to read about kids their age or a little older. Boys like to read books with boy main characters. Girls don't care.

Sidekick (optional)

You might want to include a sidekick/friend for your protagonist to bounce ideas off. Someone they can talk to. For example, in mysteries detectives often have partners they review the facts with.

Antagonist (antagonizes the protagonist)

This is the person who antagonizes the protagonist from beginning to end. Sometimes they are mere irritants like Draco Malfoy in the first Harry Potter book. Other times they are simply the bad guy out to get your hero. A bully. A murderer. The law. ETC. ETC.

"A dramatist is a congenital eavesdropper with the instincts of a Peeping Tom."

Kenneth Tynan
1927 – 1980

1.2 Setting - the "where"

This is pretty obvious. Where does the story take place? On the moon? In a small town? In the city? Or in the wilds of Alaska? The place your story unfolds should have an impact on your plot's development and your protagonist's character.

A special note for Fantasy and Sci-Fi writers. The world you create for your characters must be clear, consistent, and explained in such a way that the reader can experience it without being confused. The rules of the world must be established and maintained or your reader will be confused. The more complex your world, the harder you will have to work to make it feel real.

1.3 Time - the "when"

Another obvious point, but important. Your story can take place at any time. Present. Past. Or Future. The time period you choose, will somewhat dictate your story options. For example, cavemen didn't wear watches. Digital cameras didn't exist in the 1960s. And Genghis Khan never dated Marie Antoinette.

✏ QUICK NOTES
JOT DOWN YOUR STORY PARTICULARS

Protagonist: _____

Sidekick(optional):_____

Antagonist:_____

Setting:_____

Time:_____

BOOK JACKET DESCRIPTION

Okay, now that you have an idea of why you're writing this book, who you're writing it for and what kind of story you want it to be, it's a great time to write the book jacket description. Pretend you've finished the manuscript and want to sell it. What would appear on the back cover to make a reader want to buy it?

This exercise forces you to focus. It helps to make sure your "story idea" has enough drama to appeal to readers. It also subconsciously validates your project. Makes it real.

Most book jacket descriptions include information about your protagonist, the setting, the genre, a teaser and a strong hint of what's at stake. It does not reveal the entire plot or lay out the ending. Read a few.

Using the information from the previous exercises, write a book jacket description for your book. This is also a good time to choose a working title, even if it's just the name of your main character.

 **YOUR TURN**

YOUR WORKING BOOK TITLE

_____

✏ YOUR BOOK JACKET DESCRIPTION

"The writer probably knows what he meant when he wrote a book, but he should immediately forget what he meant when he's written it."

William Golding
1911 – 1993

THE BEGINNING Part Two

CONFLICTS

A story about a perfect person who lives a perfect life, who never makes mistakes or has problems, would make for a boring read. Part of what compels a reader to turn the page is to see what happens next. To see how the protagonist deals with what's thrown at him in spite of his personal fears and challenges. This is the "what & why" of the BEGINNING.

2.1. Inner Conflicts

What are your protagonist's personal weaknesses or fears? These fears should affect their approach to life and how they deal with difficult situations. They are also details that they usually try to hide from the world. Even from their closest friends. By the end of your story, they should have learned to face these fears.

So. Are they afraid of dogs? Do they fear abandonment because everyone they've ever loved has left them? Are they afraid they're going to die? Are they in denial?

2.2 External Conflicts

Everyone has at least one difficult person to deal with in life. It could be their spouse, their mother or a bully at school. Or any number of others: police officer, bill collector, teacher, sibling, etc.

Your character needs at least one of these irritants to complicate their life. Remember, perfect people with perfect lives are boring. It creates a nice complication is if this irritant mirrors your character's inner, unspoken fears.

2.3 The Inciting Problem

The inciting incident is thrust on you hero and will lead to the major story conflict. It's a new problem-situation that sets up the rest of the story. In other words, this problem hints at what's to come, but doesn't spill the whole enchilada. NEW PROBLEM: A boy needs a car to impress friends. His father makes him gets a job to buy the car. LATER STORY CONFLICT: His father loses his job and everything else and they end up living in the car.

 **YOUR TURN**

Fill in the information for your protagonist.

Inner Conflict

External Conflict

New Problem

LAST LOOK EXERCISE

This is a great time to do what I call the Last Look exercise. Why a last look? Because it implies that something has radically changed for your hero and that nothing will ever be the same. This short paragraph exercise forces you to include the internal conflict, external conflict and their new problem. You may discard it in your final rewrite, but for now it will help flesh out your character and transform them into a real person with real problems.

*Last Look
*Question
*Attempt to answer
*2 significant thoughts

EXAMPLE 1

Last look: Maria took one last look at her bedroom, knowing that she'd never return.

Question: Why did her mom have to take a job in New York?

Answer: The only thing adults cared about was money__ money, position, and its status.

Thought 1: When she grew up, she'd think of her children's happiness.

Thought 2: She'd never drag them away from their best friend or their dad.

Rewritten in Maria's Voice

Maria took one last look at her bedroom, knowing that she'd never return. She frowned. Why did her mom have to take a job in New York City of all places? Okay, so it was a ridiculous question. Everyone knew the only thing adults cared about was money. Money, position, and its status. When she grew up, she'd think of her children's happiness before she did something so totally stupid that it ruined the lives of everyone around her. She'd never drag them away from their best friends or from their father.

Think of all the reader has learned about Maria from one short paragraph. Plus it forces the writer to be clear and concise.

EXAMPLE 2

Last Look: Marvin took one last look at his dragon, knowing he'd have to keep her a secret.

Question: Why did people fear them so much?

Answer: Just because they breathed fire, people thought they were dangerous.

Thought 1: His older brother Abel had a dog that bite Marvin when he was three.

Thought 2: They hadn't made Abel get rid of the dog, but then Abel was their favorite son.

Rewritten in Marvin's Voice

Marvin took one last look at his tiny yellow dragon, knowing he'd have to keep her hidden. Why did people fear the harmless creatures? Just because they breathed fire didn't mean they were dangerous. Not anywhere near as dangerous as the dog his older brother Abel had when Marvin was three. It'd bit Marvin and left a gruesome scar on his chin. His parents hadn't made Abel get rid of the dog, but then Abel was their favorite son.

Think of all the reader has learned about Marvin from one short paragraph. Plus it clearly established genre.

✎ YOUR TURN - Your protagonist

Last look: _____ took one last look at

_____,

knowing that _____

_____.

Question: Why did _____

_____

Answer

Thought 1

Thought 2

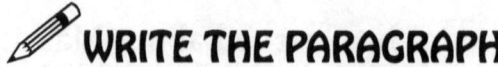 **WRITE THE PARAGRAPH**

"The best time to plan a book is while you're doing the dishes."

Agatha Christie
1890 – 1976

THE BEGINNING Part Three

STORY CONFLICT / CHALLENGE / QUEST

This is the point that the forward thrust of the story takes place. The protagonist is given a major problem to solve, an almost impossible challenge to meet or is sent on an epic quest. It's when Frodo accepted Gandalf's request to take the ring to Rivendell. It could be an athlete who decides to go for the gold and for the honor, glory and corporate sponsorships to help his destitute family. Or it might be the moment a detective is given a crime to solve.

1. Receives a challenge- external

The major story challenge is a conflict. It's something thrust upon them and not a goal that they set for themselves. Frodo's quest arrived with the appearance of Gandalf on his doorstep. The athlete is thrown into the limelight with the appearance of an Olympic talent scout. The detective is assigned his case by his captain. In all three cases, the conflict comes about from a pre-established connection that may or may not be apparent to the protagonist or the reader. Make sure it's not a coincidence. In these examples, Frodo was Bilbo's nephew and had already found the ring. The athlete already had the talent and needed to provide for his family. The detective regrets not spending time with his wife, but it's his job.

2. Debates the challenge- internal

Once the challenge arrives, have your the protagonist face an internal debate based on their personal angst. Frodo has never left the Shire. He isn't a brave hero. He doesn't have magic. The athlete is afraid no one will care for his crippled brother if he leaves. He's afraid of failure. The detective's afraid he will fail to catch the serial killer who will kill again and again.

3. Meet the antagonist

At this point, your protagonist should meet the antagonist in a revealing scene that also reveals the personal danger to your hero. Frodo slips the ring on his finger and sees the burning eye and experiences its consuming evil. The athlete is sabotaged by a fellow competitor who was a former friend. The detective receives a call from the killer that his wife will be the next victim.

✏ YOUR TURN
Fill in the information for your story.

Protagonist receives a challenge- external

Protagonist debates the challenge - internal

Meet the antagonist

REPEAT LAST LOOK EXERCISE
BIG HINT: This exercise is valuable for all major characters.

🖊 YOUR TURN - Your Antagonist

Last look: _____ took one last look at

_____ _____,

knowing that _____

Question: Why did_____

_____

Answer:

Thought 1:

Thought 2:

✏ WRITE THE PARAGRAPH

Photo Credit Michael Childers

"And all writing is creating or spinning dreams for other people so they won't have to bother doing it themselves."

Beth Henley
1952

2. THE MIDDLE Part One

The middle section of the story is the most challenging to write. It is half of your story. In this section the protagonist sets out to accomplish his goal. He makes plans to get what he wants. At the same time, the antagonist is doing the same thing.

Neither should get what they want . . . both should be frustrated, which will complicate the story plot. Each situation should escalate from the previous.

PROTAGONIST ACCEPTS THE CHALLENGE

This section starts when the protagonist accepts the challenge, either willingly or having been forced into it. He forms a plan of action and sets out to accomplish the goal/challenge. Frodo leaves the Shire. The athlete leaves his family for the Olympic Training Camp. The detective straps on his gun and hits the streets.

He will travel toward his goal in a series of scenes, each leading him closer to his objective. Try to keep the scenes interesting, realistic and dramatic. They should move the storyline forward. The progression of scenes must be compelling. To help you do this, try plotting them using the following guidelines.

When the protagonist accepts the challenge, it is the major conflict that propels the story to the end. It is more than just a reaction to what the protagonist believes about the situation.

WEAK SOLUTION ONE: Let's return to Marvin and his dragon from the Last Look exercise. Let's say Marvin runs away to protect his dragon. This is an okay plot point, but it doesn't have much of a through line to propel a novel to the end. He's not confronting or solving anything. Once he's left home, the dragon may be safe, but Marvin hasn't confronted anything. He just ran away. Yes, he could have a series of fun adventures, but . . . it is simply his reaction to the problem. He hasn't learned anything. He hasn't solved anything. It's just his knee jerk response. It might be enough for a short story, but it's not enough to be the main conflict of the story.

WEAK SOLUTION TWO: Marvin is captured and taken to dragon school with his dragon. Again, this is an okay plot point, but he still doesn't have to make any big decisions. There's not a major issue he has to deal with, unless you embellish and take it to the next step. As it reads, he might learn how to handle his dragon, but it's not a quest on its own. Like the previous weak example, it's not enough on its own to sustain a powerful novel.

A STRONG MAJOR CONFLICT: Marvin's brother is taken hostage and with the aide of his dragon, Marvin must rescue Abel from the evil northern Dragon Warlord who wants control over all dragons and the Kingdom of Urrrdong. Remember, Abel was the favored son, treated like a prince and Marvin like a slave. To save his brother, Marvin has to act, plan, come to grips with his jealousy of Abel and overcome his fear of heights. This is a big enough problem to carry a story from start to finish. It has a specific goal, i.e. SAVE ABEL. He can run away to accomplish this. He can end up in Dragon school, too. But he has a clear objective. As the story progresses, the end goal may enlarge to include saving the Kingdom, but the initial goal of saving Abel doesn't change.

✎ YOUR TURN
Write your protagonist's major conflict / challenge.

1 – 2 – 3 * With a Twist!

I'm sure you're familiar with the following three tales. Look at them and note how things seem to happen in 3's. For some reason "three" is a satisfying number. It's true in flower arranging, in art and when plotting scenes . . . as long as they end with a twist and something a little unexpected.

GOLDILOCKS & THE THREE BEARS

Goldilocks checks out the house. . .

1. PORRIDGE:
Too cold!   Too Hot!   Just right.   EATS IT ALL

2. CHAIRS:
Too hard!   Too soft!   Just right.   BREAKS CHAIR

3. BEDS:
Too hard! Too soft! Just right.   GOES TO SLEEP

Enter the bears. . .

1.Someone's been eating my porridge.
. . . and ate it all up.

2. Someone's been sitting in my chair.
. . . and broke it all up

3. Someone's been sleeping in my bed.
. . . and here she is.

THE THREE LITTLE PIGS

BUILD 3 HOUSES:
1. Straw   2. Sticks   3. Bricks

WOLF: Huffs & puffs 3 TIMES
1st & 2nd huffs: first two houses destroyed,

3rd huff: the brick house stands firm

.

THE WIZARD OF OZ

MEETS 3 COMPANIONS:
1. Scarecrow   2.Tin Man   3.Cowardly Lion

MAKES 3 ATTEMPTS TO SEE THE WIZARD:
1. Delayed
2. Told no.
3. Let in, but given a task.

SEES THE WICKED WITCH 3 TIMES BEFORE ENGAGING
1. When Dorothy first arrives
2. Just before meeting the Tin Man
3. In the Emerald City

You could find more examples of 3's, but. . .
Remember to think about 3's when you're plotting.

"A writer is congenitally unable to tell the truth and that is why we call what he writes fiction."

William Faulkner
1897 – 1962

THE MIDDLE Part One Continued

1.1 Protagonist Forms a Plan of Action

The three little pigs leave home. They want independence. They each build a house and plan to live long, happy and secure lives on their own. The third little pig is our protagonist.

1.2. The Plan Goes Wrong

The wolf arrives. He's our antagonist. He blows down the straw and stick houses. The two pigs are forced to move in with their brother in his brick house and they're all stuck living together again.

1.3 Protagonist Makes New Plans

The third pig makes plans to get rid of the wolf and his guests. He forces his bothers do all the housework so they will want to leave while he plots to trick the wolf into taking a trip to the Bahamas.

Depending on the length of your story, these scenes will repeat. In the shortest story this should happen at least three times.

🖉 YOUR TURN
Plot the next three scenes of your story.

Protagonist Forms a Plan of Action

The Plan Goes Wrong

Protagonist Makes New Plans

Again the Protagonist Forms a Plan of Action

Again the Plan Goes Wrong

Again the Protagonist Makes New Plans

Again the Protagonist Forms a Plan of Action

Again the Plan Goes Wrong

Again the Protagonist Makes New Plans

"For a long time now I have tried simply to write the best I can. Sometimes I have good luck and write better than I can."

Ernest Hemingway
1899 – 1961

THE MIDDLE Part Two
MID-POINT EPIPHANY - Ah ha!

Halfway through the middle, the protagonist must have an epiphany, a new insight about herself or her quest. For example, a girl realizes even thought she isn't drop-dead gorgeous, she isn't hideous either. This will change her inner attitude and her approach to completing her task, but the goal will remain the same. This will be the result of a dramatic life change that you throw in their path. She has a fight with her "pretty" sister only to learn that her sister was always jealous of her. One door opens as another door closes.

2.1 Recognize flawed perspective

Something happens, preferably something totally unexpected, to change the protagonist's view of life. Often it's connected to either his inner fear or external fear. He sees the bully as pathetic instead of threatening. Or the insecure female detective finds out the man she's dating is a murderer. Or, maybe the kid who thinks he's a jinx to all his friends, realizes that he isn't when a flood wipes out their home. After all, he can't control the weather. This means that their bad luck can't be his fault.

2.2 Come to terms with fears

Once the hero understands her fears have been unrealistic she must re-evaluate herself. The female detective comes to understand that she doesn't have to settle for just any man, and especially not the murderer who dumped her. The child frightened of the bully now sees his tormentor as a pathetic frightened loser and has sympathy for him. The kid who's afraid to let people close to him because he might bring them bad luck, now is free to make friends again.

2.3 Renewed energy, same goal

Your protagonist is more confident. Is more determined than ever to finish the job. The third little pig no longer longs for his two brother pigs to move out, but he still wants to get the wolf. Cinderella no longer feels alone because she has her fairy godmother, but she still wants to go to the ball and meet the prince. I may still be short, but being short has its advantages and I still want to finish this book.

✏ YOUR TURN

What happened to make your protagonist recognize their flawed perspective?

Come to terms with fears

Renewed energy, same goal

"When I was a little boy, they called me a liar, but now that I am grown up, they call me a writer."

Isaac Bashevis Singer
1902 – 1991

THE MIDDLE Part Three
GOES FOR IT MORE DETERMINED

This second half of the middle becomes more exciting because the protagonist is more determined than ever and is willing to take even greater risks than in the beginning. This will up the ante, increase the excitement and add even more potential danger to your hero. The detective's wife is now the serial killer's next target. The heroine realizes she's hopelessly engaged to the wrong man because she loves another.

3.1 Change of Attitude

This all starts with a change of attitude. The protagonist refuses to be helpless or a victim any longer. They become empowered with their new found confidence. They may also have changed an opinion about someone or a situation. The environmental protestor comes to realize he is wasting paper with his handout flyers and the sign he holds. A wife is trying to find out why she's not happy in her perfect marriage. Then she realizes her husband has been having an affair. It's a shock.

3.2 New Focused Plan of Attack

Armed with new confidence, the protagonist resumes his quest. He has a better understanding of both himself and the situation. This allows him to focus more clearly on what he needs to do to win. The protestor still wants to save the environment so he writes a song to get his message out. The wife realizes the marriage will never be perfect and her happiness will come with a divorce.

3.3 Realizes Bigger Importance of Challenge

The protagonist comes to understand that what he's set out to accomplish is more important than he realized in the beginning. His success or lack of success will impact others. This is when Marvin realizes the evil magician wants to take over the kingdom and to rule with ruthless abandon. If Marvin fails, there's more than just him, his brother and his dragon's fates at stake.

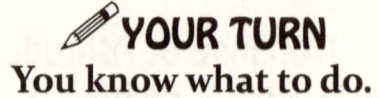

YOUR TURN
You know what to do.

What's your protagonist's change of attitude?

What's her new focused plan of attack?

What's the "bigger importance" of her challenge?

"The secret of good writing is to say an old thing in a new way or to say a new thing in an old way."

Richard Harding Davis
1864 – 1916

THE END Part One
THE CLIMAX

The End takes up the last 1/4 of the story. The whole book has been leading up to this moment when the protagonist faces off with the antagonist. You don't want to rush it or leave out the final physical and emotional steps taken by your hero. It should be the dramatic fulfillment of your main character's quest.

1.1 Point of No Return

At the beginning of the end, your protagonist should feel that he has reached the point of no retreat. He's changed and will never be the same. He's set things in motion that can't be erased or undone. He has to move forward even though everything he's worked for up to this point feels doomed to fail. Frodo continues to climb Mount Doom even though he fears he's fated to fail.

2.2 Blackest Moment

Something happens to convince your protagonist his task is doomed. There's no chance of success. He emotionally gives up, but continues to work toward his goal even though he expects failure. This is called the blackest moment. This could be the moment when a mother who's scrambled to earn the money necessary for her child's operation, learns that the condition has advanced and it's too late. The doctor refuses to perform the surgery because there is only a one in a billion chance it might succeed. The mother won't take no. She hunts for another doctor who will operate even though she knows her son's condition is hopeless.

2.3 Moral Decision

The protagonist has a moral decision to make in what seems like a no-win situation.

If they do the right thing, they believe they will lose everything.

If they do the wrong thing they can win, but at a high cost.

If they do anything it will have a negative consequence.

If they do nothing, it will have a negative consequence.

After fighting with their conscience and deliberating between what is the right thing to do and what would be the wrong thing to do, the protagonist finds renewed strength from within. This strength should come from a memory or an experience. This allows him to makes what he thinks will be the best choice of action.

Detective Morley's moral decision might be whether to arrest the serial killer or to blow his brains out to make sure he'll never hurt another person. As a cop, he believes in the due process of law. He also knows the killer is rich, will buy his freedom and move to another country to kill again.

✎ YOUR TURN
Answer the following.

What is her point of no return?

What is her blackest moment?

What is her moral sticking point?

If she does the right thing, what do she believe they will lose?

If she do the wrong thing, what does she think she can win? But at what high cost?

If she does anything, what negative consequence does she think it will have?

If she does nothing, what negative consequence does she think it will have?

"A good novel tells us the truth about its hero; but a bad novel tells us the truth about its author."

Gilbert K. Chesterton
1874 – 1936

THE END Part Two
PERSONAL SHOWDOWN

2.1 Face Personal Problem

In the beginning, your protagonist had a personal problem that was somewhat debilitating. This is the place where he faces and overcome his fear of this area of his life. Although Ron is a secondary character in the Harry Potter series, he has a huge fear of spiders. He is called upon to rise above this personal fear to help Harry escape from the giant spiders in the forest. He doesn't lose his fear, but he does face it.

2.2 Confront Major Problem

No more delays, the time has arrived to confront the major challenge your protagonist set out to solve from the beginning. He needs to come up with a plan or strategy to make it happen. I wrote a book set in 1946 about a boy who lives with his grandparents in Hawaii. When his grandparents disappear and his best friend is arrested as a leper, he sets out to find his birth parents on a neighboring island. He has several adventures, learns some difficult truths, but never gives up his search for his parents. Not even when it means risking his own death.

2.3. Go All Out to Fight the Foe

The protagonist sets his plan into action. Everything is on the line and there's no backing down. He's willing to risk it all. Marvin, the dragon boy, has devised a plan to rescue his brother from the evil sorcerer's dungeon. He's enlisted the help of some other characters he's met during the course of the story. Plus he will rely on the help of his dragon to fly him to the tower in the center of the compound. From there he will climb down and open a secret passage hidden in the cunning magician's bedroom. Marvin's cohorts will join him. They will storm the dungeon and free his brother. The plan is risky, but it's the only one that's viable. He sets out at daybreak.

YOUR TURN

Face Personal Problem

Confront Major external Problem

Go All Out to Fight the Foe

"I'm like a big old hen. I can't cluck too long about the egg I've just laid because I've got five more inside me pushing to get out."

Louis L'Amour
1908 – 1988

THE END Part Three
RESOLUTION & WRAP-UP

3.1 Showdown

The plan is set in motion. It leads the protagonist to a showdown with the antagonist. This is the scene at the end when the protagonist faces their personal problems and confronts the challenge of the major conflict. It should be BIG and DRAMATIC and SURPRISING. Avoid clichéd dramatic endings, unless you can give it an intriguing twist.

3.2 Resolve major challenge

The protagonist must solve or win the story conflict through thought and action!!! It's her story. Her problem. Her solution. Do not allow another character to take away her glory by stepping in a solving the problem for the protagonist. No act of God. No well meaning savior. No parent stopping the bullying.

3.3 Wrap up lose ends

Every problem you raised in the beginning must be addressed. This is called the resolution of the plot. It's when the reader learns what's happened and why it happened. Once this is complete, it's time to wrap-up the story and to bring it to a satisfying end.

Sometimes authors will "book end" their opening and ending scenes. They revisit a beginning situation with a different and pithier conclusion.

And they all lived happily after . . . or hopefully

something better. Remember, the last sentence should put the story and the protagonist's struggle in perspective without sounding preachy. It's also the sentence that will sell your next book.

YOUR TURN

Describe the Showdown Scene

Resolve major challenge

Wrap up any lose ends and any questions readers might have gleaned along the way.

Resolution

Final Wrap Up & Goodbye to the characters

✏ Story Planning Checklist

In the beginning . . .

_____ Starts with a hook.
_____ Protagonist
_____ Personal problem
_____ Physical description
_____ Setting
_____ Major conflict / challenge
_____ Antagonist

In the middle . . .

_____ Accepts the conflict challenge
_____ Series of failed plans
       [action + reaction + new plan]
_____ Epiphany
_____ Series of wiser plans
       [action + reaction + new plan]

In the end . . .

_____ Climax
_____ Moral decision
_____ Showdown
_____ Resolution
_____ Wrap-up

Now you're ready to write!

Remember, the plan is a just a plan.

It can be changed as you write. But when one story point changes, it can dramatically change the rest of your story. If it does, you'll have to GO BACK and adjust your story plan.

HURRAY YOUR PLOT IS DONE!

Now a few words about starting your first draft.

You have your book plotted! Yeah! It's time to start writing.

I will admit I spend a lot of time on my first few chapters before I jump into my story. Partially because the story doesn't seem real until I start writing it. Three issues seem to crop up if I don't take the time to do this.

One. Sometimes my characters have a mind of their own and resist my coaching. They want the story to go in a slightly different direction. Or they don't want to be afraid of spiders.

Two. I need a killer opening paragraph (last look). I know I can rewrite it later, and probably will, but I want it to be good when I start. Subconsciously it sets the standard for the book. If I don't take the time to get it right at first, I will lose interest in the project.

Three. I need time to settle into my imagined characters' minds, into their imagined world and truly understand their issues. I have to know these things well before I can write their story. Plus I need to give myself permission to go back and re-tweak my plot if for some reason it doesn't feel right after I've begun.

WARNING! Don't spend forever, or you'll never write the book.

Once I'm in the skin of my protagonist I finish writing the first draft. I don't care about the typos. The mistakes. Poor grammar. Weak dialogues. I can fix them later. I hope you caught that.

I SAID, FIRST DRAFT.

You've just started molding the block of clay. When it's finished, the real work begins. The cleaning, tightening and tweaking.

OPENING PARAGRAPH

Let's go back to the LAST LOOK paragraphs you wrote for your protagonist. Upon rereading it you might be tempted to use it for your first paragraph. However, "I took my last look at . . . " is probably not the most powerful first sentence you can write to hook your reader. It could be good, but if 10,000 other writers read this book and start their books with, "I TOOK MY LAST LOOK. . . ," it will morph into a clichéd kind of "DARK AND STORY NIGHT" first line. It's time to look for a better first line or lines. Let's go back to Marvin and his dragon. Here are a few opening lines that might hook a reader. They all set different tones for different kind of books.

Marvin bumped his arm and winced. Dragon bites take forever to heal, he thought and studied the gruesome scar that had started to turn green on his wrist.

Or

Marvin sensed eyes watching him and couldn't control the burning shiver that crept up his spine. He scanned the surrounding trees and the low dense scrub brush.

"Who's there?" he asked in a hoarse whisper.

Or

The third moon of Ashtar sat on the Eastern-horizon. Marvin had to hurry. He was late. The Guild's Apprentice Choosing had already begun.

I am Marvin, the great and powerful. The favorite son of the village chieftain. Heir to the throne. Heir to untold riches. Okay, so I lied. My name is Marvin and my only claim to fame is . . . well, a little too embarrassing to share. Instead, let me tell you about my pet dragon.

These four openings create four different expectations for the reader. One is the beginning of a funny story. One is the beginning of an epic fantasy tale. One is the beginning of a mysterious, secretive story. One is the beginning of a boy's coming of age transformation.

Only you can decide what kind of a story you want to write. Readers decide what kind of stories they want to read. To make them happy, you have to give them the story they're expecting. BEWARE of writing an exciting beginning that doesn't match the book you're writing.

How do I know this? Been there, done that. I have a manuscript sitting in my computer that started out as a funny book and halfway through morphed into a Mary Higgins Clark creepy mystery for middle grade readers. It was about a serious subject and I mistakenly thought that I'd handle the topic with a protagonist who had a weird sense of humor.

My boy Howie is the younger brother of a boy who'd disappeared five years earlier. Howie is desperate for his parents' attention because all they seemed to care about is his missing brother. He tries all sorts of zany things to get them to notice him. All laugh-out-loud funny. Halfway through the book his brother's remains are found. Howie's mid-point epiphany is the realization that to earn his parents' respect by tracking down the person responsible for his brother's murder.

Goodbye funny story.

Hello disappointed reader. They picked up a funny book for light entertainment and halfway through were slammed with a dark kidnapping murder mystery. Needless to say, it never went to print.

So, keep in mind the kind of book you want to create and then write an exciting opening for it. Still need more help? Go back and reread the opening paragraphs of the books you loved. Next go the library and read the opening paragraphs of books printed in the last ten years. Analyze both the ones that make you want to read more and the ones you're glad you didn't buy.

Use your last look paragraph as a resource and starting point to rewrite your opening.

The following pages are writing-craft advice to help you with your rewrite.

"Only a mediocre writer is always at his best."

W. Somerset Maugham
1874 – 1965

A FEW WORDS ABOUT CRAFT

Regardless of one's writing style, there are rules that the writer needs to follow. Most of you should already know the obvious. Capitalize the first word of a sentence. Dialogue is contained in quotation marks. Etc. Etc. If you need help with basic grammar, there are several books out there. Don't rely on the automatic spell and grammar checker in your word processing program. It makes mistakes.

The NINE (3 X 3) additional areas you need to master have more to do with your word choice rather than any specific grammatical rule. Don't worry about correcting them while writing your first draft, but look for them to tweak in the second. The more you're aware of these writing boo boos, the more streamlined your writing will become. Over time you will commit fewer of them in your first drafts.

P.O.V.

P.O.V. is short for POINT OF VIEW. A story, or sections of the story, should be told from a single P.O.V. Unless your character can read minds, they can't know what the other characters are thinking. They can only guess. As the author, it's important that you don't shift P.O.V.'s midstream.

Example of 1st Person P.O.V. Shift:

I walked into the crowded room looking for my boyfriend. He spotted me first and waved me over. He thought I looked hot.

P.O.V. shift from I to him.

See the problem? It should be obvious. "I'm" telling the story at first and then "he" has an inner thought.

2 possible re-writes from a single P.O.V.

He smiled and I could tell he liked my new hot look.

He whistled and said, "You look hot."

Example of 3rd person P.O.V. Shift:

Amanda walked into the room wishing she hadn't let herself be talked into the blind date. What had she been thinking? That she'd find Mr. Right in cyberspace? Not likely. Hesitantly she looked around the room. He saw her first and waved her over. His Blind-Date Fairy Godfather must be in a good mood. SHE was hotter than hot.

P.O.V. shift from her to him

2 possible re-writes from a single P.O.V.

The guy was obviously a dork. He was grinning like he'd won the dating lottery. Too bad she'd lost. Again.

From her blind date's nervous twitches and silly grin, it was obvious he didn't get out much.

✏ YOUR TURN
Spot the P.O.V shift and fix.

The dog watched his master through the window. He whined and gave a little bark. Look at me. Look at me. Let me in. I want my dog biscuits. John swore. Didn't the stupid dog know he worked nights? He pressed a pillow to his ear and tried to go back to sleep.

VOICE

VOICE is the personality of your story's narrator. Whether you're writing in first person or third, voice is what makes your book unique. It sets the tone. It reveals the kind of story you're writing: intimate and personal or distant and reserved. It should help the reader connect with your protagonist. Most importantly, it should remain constant. I'm currently working on a project told from two separate first person P.O.V.'s in alternating chapters.

Hopefully you'll be able to see that each has a unique voice. The opening paragraphs, the sentence structures and word choices are different. They should set totally different character expectations.

SERENA'S VOICE

I stared at the monitor and blinked hard. It felt like some invisible hand had seized my throat, which was totally ridiculous. I was alone in the room. Just Unix, Macintosh and me.

On the screen, a news article had popped up, marking the ten-year anniversary of a tragic hit-and-run accident. The photo of a mangled dark blue SUV dominated the page. Unconsciously my hand felt for the small scar over my right temple. The forgotten odors of spilled petrol and oil slammed my senses. I gagged. My eyes watered as I swallowed hard to push down the unbidden bile.

The sensible thing would have been to click off, but I hadn't seen this story before.

J.T.'S VOICE

I stood at the self check-in machine and waited for my boarding pass to print. My mom hovered like an annoying mosquito.

"You've got your passport?" she asked for the zillionth time.

I pulled it from the back pocket of my school slacks and waved it at her.

"You shouldn't keep it in your back pocket. You could lose it." She straightened my red striped Christian Academy School tie.

Talking about losing something, I planned to lose the tie as soon as I was out of her sight.

The automated machine spit out my boarding pass. I snatched it and grinned. In a few minutes, no more "Mom advice" for a whole week. I couldn't wait.

✐ YOUR TURN

Write the beginning sentence of your story using 2 different voices.

"The difference between the right word and almost the right word is the difference between lightning and the lightning bug."

Mark Twain
1835 – 1910

ACTIVE V.S. PASSIVE WRITING

Active writing is strong. Passive writing is weak. So what's the difference? Passive writing wastes paper by using three or four weak words when one strong word would be better.

The classic passive combo to avoid overusing is:

was + verb(ing) + adverb(ly)

Passive Example 1:
I was walking slowly.

Why not use a descriptive verb instead? If you're stuck for the perfect word, use your Thesaurus.

I ambled. I strolled. I sauntered. I wandered. I moseyed.

✏ YOUR TURN
Rewrite the sentence five times replacing the passive combination with a strong verb.

I hurriedly was walking quickly home.

1.

2.

3.

4.

5.

Good job! Does this mean you should never use "was," an "ing" verb or an "ly" adverb? No it does not. But use them judiciously, not twenty times on the same page.

In the seventh grade I had to memorize the various forms of the verb "to be." These words are like "was" when combined with an active verb ending in "ing."

is am are was were

has have had

do does did

be being been

shall will should would

may might must can could

So pay attention and see if you can replace them with an active verb.

✎ YOUR TURN

Rewrite the following from passive to active. If necessary, use two sentences.

Fred is thinking about his newspaper.

I am wondering why my husband is late.

Jonus and Marcus were having an argument.

I can't stop thinking about the day I was bit by a dog.

This next one is tricky. It needs a set up sentence before it's rewrite.

Monica might be having an asthma attack.

REWRITE:
Monica's face turned blue. Was she having an asthma attack?

✏️ YOUR TURN
Rewrite with a set up sentence.

Sally must be thinking about her new dress.

SHOW! DON'T TELL!

This is a big one. If you've written for very long or are in a serious critique group, I'm sure you've heard, "SHOW! DON'T TELL!" I think I'll let my "TELL EXAMPLES" show you the difference.

Tell Example 1:

John came into the room. He was drunk.

Show:

John stumbled into the room, knocking over a plant stand that crashed to the floor. He reeked of alcohol. "Wuz, happening?" he said, his words slurred together in a bad Elvis impression.

Tell Example 2:

I was really nervous. I hadn't studied for the test.

Show:

The tardy bell rang and I slipped into my seat at the back of the classroom. I fumbled in my purse for a pen, my hands damp and trembling. A casual observer might think I had Parkinson's. That is if sixteen-year-olds get the disease. I wasn't sure. My stomach joined the sick act and I tasted bile. I tried to swallow, but my mouth felt like an ancient mummy's. Why hadn't I studied? This test made up fifty percent of my biology grade.

Tell Example 3:

Mary insulted me.

Show:

"You don't really think you'll make the cheerleading team," Mary said. "You're not the type."

"What type?" I asked, regretting the words as soon as they'd slipped from my lips.

"The cool type." Then she gave me what looked like a pity smile. "You do realize you're pathetic. Just like your retarded brother."

She'd gone too far. It was one thing to make fun of me. I could fight back. Tommy couldn't.

✏ YOUR TURN

Transform the following "tells" into "shows."

1. Maggie couldn't understand what the man wanted, because what he said didn't make sense.

2. Marc was a really, really good basketball player.

3. The girl looked happy and excited to play with her new doll.

REPETITION V.S. VARIETY

We all have words and fallback phrases we like to use. Sometimes we like them so much, we use them over and over. Unless you are repeating the words for special emphasis, it's not a good idea. Marc Antony in Shakespeare's play Julius Caesar repeats the phrase, "good and honorable men," several times during his eulogy for Caesar. Each time he repeats the phrase, the words take on new meaning. It's intentional and well thought.

Other times we are just lazy. Every time our character is embarrassed, their face "turns red" or "blazes with heat." Repeated thirty or forty times in a single story is a bit much. It's okay to write them in your first draft, but when rewriting change them up. An easy way to spot them is to use the "find" feature that most computer writing programs list under editing.

Of course, there are certain words you will repeat and cannot avoid.

Articles like "the," "an" & "a."

The words "asked" & "said."

Your characters' names.

Pronouns like "he", "she", "it", "they" & "them."

These you get a free pass to use as often as necessary. Two words you will use often, but can overuse, are "and" and "but."

"And" Overuse Example:

I can't wait to go camping and go swimming. We will also get to eat Smores, hot dogs and chili. I've already packed my sleeping bag and clothes. Plus, my two best friends are going with us, Maggie and Freda. It's going to be a fun and exciting trip.

Rewrite:

Maggie, Freda and I are going camping with my parents. Dad's already packed our camping gear. Mom's bought all sorts of great food for the week. I think I'll enjoy the Smores the best. Freda is a real hot dog nut. Maggie just loves chili. Of course, we'll have to wait at least an hour after we eat before we can swim in the lake. I can't wait! It's going be awesome.

Same basic information with only one "and."

"But" Overuse Example:

Thomas wanted to go home, but his mom said he had to stay until the end of the week. She might as well have said forever. He wouldn't have minded the visit, but his grandparents didn't have T.V. or Internet. There was only one other kid on the island, but she was a girl and pretty much useless in his mind. He mom said he was prejudiced, but he said he wasn't.

Rewrite:

Thomas wanted to go home. His mom said he had to stay until the end of the week. She might as well have said forever. He wouldn't have minded the visit, but his grandparents didn't have T.V. or Internet. There was only one other kid on the island and she was a girl. That made her pretty much useless in his mind.

"There's nothing wrong with having a girl for a friend," his mom said.

"Unless she thinks she's your girlfriend." He snagged a rock, threw it into the pond and watched it skip to the other side. "I'd rather eat worms."

I wanted to go to the concert, but I was afraid I'd get lost and never find my way home again. Kind of like a Hansel and Gretel moment, but in modern times. I just love fairy tales and mysteries and suspense and romance. I like romance the best, but only if they have happy endings. Maybe I could find romance and a fairy tale happy ending at the concert, but it wasn't likely.

The last kind of repetition I want to mention is when you repeat the same word in a paragraph numerous times when you should have substituted a better word. A more powerful word that lends additional description to the action or scene you're spinning for the reader. Unless someone else reads your work out loud to you, it's easy to miss these kinds of repeats.

Example:

I raced down the street chased by a pack of dogs. They raced after me, barking. The street was wet. I slipped and slowed as I tried to catch my balance. The dogs grew closer and it looked like I would end up dog food. I almost was ready to give up when a big black car raced down the street toward me. It screeched to a stop. The passenger door flew open. I jumped in.

"I" x 6 + "street" x 3 + "raced x 3" + "dog/s" x 3 = too many repetitions

The Rewrite:

I raced down the street chased by a pack of dogs. They bounded after me, barking and snarling. The pavement was wet, causing me to slip. The vicious curs grew closer and it looked like I would end up Kibbles and Bits. A big black car turned onto the boulevard traveling at a high speed. It screeched to a stop just inches from my feet. The passenger door flew open. I jumped in.

"I" x 3　　　　　"street" x 1　"raced" x 1　"dog/s" x 1

SIDE NOTE

Whether I'm editing on the computer or on a paper hardcopy, I like to use a highlighter to mark REPEAT errors. It's a real visual shocker when you see a dozen or more yellow-correction-bricks on the page. Sometimes I get creative and use a different color to mark my PASSIVE errors. A third color for my TELLS. A fourth for P.O.V shifts. More than once I've ended up with a pretty interesting looking modern-art mosaic.

✒ YOUR TURN
Rewrite the following.

Ralph hated his name. The kids at school said Ralph sounded like barf, but his mom said the name Ralph was his great-great-grandfather's who was a war hero. Ralph should be proud of the name and wear it like a medal. That was easier said than done and Ralph pleaded with her to change his name to John or Doug or to any other normal sounding name. A name that kids wouldn't tease him about all the time, because didn't she know the kids at his school were so mean.

AUTHOR INTRUSION

I've been guilty of this one big time. More times than I wish to admit. AUTHOR INTRUSION is when you tell the reader how to interpret what you've written. It reads like you didn't trust them to have a brain or know how to use it. OUCH! Now that is harsh.

I believe when writers do this, it is a subconscious manifestation that they don't trust their own writing.

It's a weird combination of telling and showing. You may have written the perfect scene, but you just don't trust your reader to get it. I'm going to use an earlier example to demonstrate what I mean.

Author Intrusion Example:

The tardy bell rang and I slipped into my seat at the back of the classroom. I fumbled in my purse for a pen, my hands damp and trembling. A casual observer might think I had Parkinson's. My hypochondriac stomach joined the sick act and I tasted bile. I tried to swallow, but my mouth was dry like desert sand. This test made up fifty percent of my biology grade. Why hadn't I studied? I was nervous and afraid I'd fail.

In the last sentence I, the author, is telling you, the reader, what to think. . . that the character was nervous and afraid of failure. This is totally unnecessary.

Your job as the author is to write the scene and let the reader interpret it.

SUSPENSE V.S. SURPRISE

Surprise is when something happens without pre-warning. A bomb explodes in a busy shopping mall. Too many "surprises" in a story is like a chase scene in a movie that goes on-and-on until you start wishing the hero will plow into the next piling and die.

Suspense is when the reader expects the bomb to go off, hopes it won't, and fears for the life of the potential victims. Suspense will drive a story and can be used over and over again. It adds urgency to scenes and stories, making them exciting. And it compels the reader to continue reading. There are three time-tested-techniques writers use to create suspense.

1. THE TICKING TIME BOMB

One is the ticking time bomb. Something big is at stake, like the end of the world. The hero only has five days to find the alien space station and disable it before the creatures destroy all humankind.

2. CLUEING IN THE READER

The reader is clued in on a dangerous situation that's about to happen, but the characters in the book are clueless. While some editors shun prologues, they are effective in creating suspense. It's night. The serial killer is outside the bedroom window of a young woman, watching. We see the glint of a knife in his hand. The bedroom light goes out. The man quickly retreats to the back of the house. A car pulls up outside the house. The man slides back into the cover of darkness and disappears. Chapter one opens with the woman happily cooking breakfast in her kitchen. We know the killer will return, we just don't know when.

You could write the same description within a single scene, but this time your protagonist is the woman inside the house. Of course, the outcome of this scene will be different, because she is the protagonist and the hero. In both cases, the writer clues in the reader, but keeps the protagonist in the dark.

3. MULTIPLE P.O.V.'s

Often romance stories are told from two points of view__ hers and his. This gives the writer plenty of opportunity to set up scenes with the potential for disastrous results. From her P.O.V. we know she's deadly afraid of dogs. From his P.O.V. we know he's bought her a puppy to win her love. The results can be funny, sad or poignant depending on the kind of story you're writing.

🖉 YOUR TURN

Write the same scene three ways. Take note how the tone, voice and suspense are altered.

1. Set the stage by writing a suspenseful prologue to your book in third person. (He or she saw . . .)

2. Rewrite your prologue into a suspenseful scene that would be contained in your book using first person narrative. (I saw. . .)

3. Write the scene again, from two entirely different points of view. The first P.O.V. sets up the situation and triggers the suspense revealed by the second P.O.V.

CLICHÉS

It's a dark and stormy night raining cats and dogs, but that's okay because I knew that all's well that ends well. Of course you don't want to break the bank trying to teach an old dog new tricks. That would be like trying to paddle upstream without a paddle. . . I could go on, but I'll spare you.

Clichés are those phrases that we all know so well. We've heard them a million times and when push comes to shove, we pull them out without thinking. Oops, I just did it again.

Usually it's a good idea to avoid clichés when you write. There are two exceptions I can think of to use them. One is if it's a personality trait of one of your secondary characters. The other exception is more fun. It's when you fracture the cliché.

Example 1:
You can't teach an old dog new tricks.

I looked at my husband thinking that his new secretary had better not try to teach the old dog any new tricks or I'd be investing the alimony in a new house on the French Riviera.

Example 2:
It wasn't my cup of tea.

I wished I hadn't come. Having polite conversation about the break-up with my soon to be ex-mother-in-law wasn't my cup of Earl Gray.

✏ YOUR TURN
Fracture the following clichés.

Scraping the bottom of the barrel.

The apple of his eye.

In the doghouse.

The way to a man's heart is through his stomach.

When pigs fly.

He's a little wet behind the ears.

A babe in the woods.

Keep your head above water.

Let sleeping dogs lie.

A bee in her bonnet.

Caught between a rock and a hard place.

Bit off more than you can chew.

DIALOGUE

Dialogue is conversation between two people. It should not be a series of speeches. It shouldn't be used to as an info-dump for information you were too lazy to weave into the story. It should reveal your characters' personalities, emotions and coping skills. If it doesn't sound natural, it will feel stilted and phony.

So how do you make your dialogue sound real? A good place to start is to go to a coffee shop or a cafe with a notebook in hand. Sit there, pretend to be writing and eavesdrop. Write down the conversations you overhear verbatim.

You should discover that people usually fail to follow the rules of good grammar or good manners.

They often talk in fragmented sentences.

"Want to go the movies tonight?" he asked.

~~"Yes. I want to go to the movies with you this evening."~~

"Sure," I said.

They interrupt.

"Where have you been?" my mother asked.

I glanced at the clock. It was midnight, two hours after my curfew. "I went to the," I started to explain, but she cut me off.

"Do you have any idea of what time it is? You're grounded."

They don't always pay attention to what the other person is talking about and respond as such.

"Do you have any idea how worried I've been?" Mom asked.

"I'm sorry." I blinked back tears. "James was in an accident. They took him to the hospital, but_"

"Your selfish and irresponsible behavior has to stop. Do you understand?"

They avoid answering direct questions.

She leaned closer and I could smell the Johnny Walker. "Mom, you promised to quit. Where's the bottle?"

"Now that you're sixteen, you think you're all grown up." She snorted a bitter laugh. "Talk about promises. Your father made promises he never intended to keep."

They talk at cross-purposes.

"Mom, James is. . ."

"You're just like him. Selfish to the core. You think you're in love? That James is the one. Let me tell you something about love. I thought your father was the one and look where that's got me."

Tears streamed down my face. I couldn't hold them back any longer.

"Go ahead and cry." Mom's words were slurred. "It doesn't change anything. Never does."

"He's dead."

They try to change subjects when they're uncomfortable rather than directly state their true feelings.

Mom grabbed me in a bear hug and patted my back like she was trying to burp me. "Tomorrow we'll go to the mall and buy you a new outfit. How does that sound?"

✎ YOUR TURN
Write a short dialogue following the above rules.

A FINAL WORD

Congratulations, you've reached the end. Before you go, one final piece of advice.

I have no idea who said it first, but it's a phrase that bears repeating. "Rules are made for breaking." On occasion I intentionally break the rules of good grammar. Write fragments. And start sentences with "but" or "and." End a sentence with a pronoun, just because.

Make sure the rules you break are intentional and not accidental.

Hopefully the information and assignments in this book have been helpful. They work for me. They may not all work for you, but you won't know if you don't give them a try. Use them. Adapt them. Lose the ones that don't work.

Again, feel free to photocopy the pages for your personal use, but not for classroom or workshop groups.

GOOD LUCK!

Utilizing perseverance, hard work, and self-discipline you can finish a great manuscript: a short story, novella or a novel.

NOW . . .

GO

FORTH
AND

WRITE ON!

ACKNOWLEDGEMENTS

Thanks to my critque experts Sue Wyshynksi and
Christine Sackey.

ALSO BY S.D. BROWN

The Lake Quilt Mystery
The Scrapbook Riddle
Pretty Little Rumors
Host Your Own Murder Mystery Party:
DEATH AT CASINO REVEL

WRITING AS
SPIKE BROWN

Escape to Molokai
Saving Bigfoot Valley
The Royal Historian of Oz

BLOG: kidsmysteryreviews.com

www.ingramcontent.com/pod-product-compliance
Lightning Source LLC
Chambersburg PA
CBHW050502290526
45786CB00006B/2398